Breaking Through the Pain of the Past
Philippians 2:13

A Date with My Father

Sebrina D. Mays

A Date With My Father
Breaking Through the Pain of the Past

Sebrina D. Mays
sebrina.mays@gmail.com

ISBN: 978-1-949027-61-7
Printed in the USA

Published by: DestinedToPublish.com | (773) 783-2981

Dedication

My loving parents, Bernice and the late Richard, Jr.: Thank you for being not only a mother and a father to me and my siblings but also “Mommy and Daddy.” I am so thankful to God for you, ***true builders*** *of your generation.* Thank you for every building block you gave me and my siblings, enabling us to become productive members of society.

My husband of 30 years, Mark, who loves me unconditionally: Thank you for your patience and giving heart as you walked alongside me on this journey.

With Love,
Sebrina

Acknowledgements

I thank my heavenly Father for allowing me to join the family of God and receive the gift of the Holy Spirit through his son, Jesus Christ. I am honored that he called me to this task to share my story so that others could be set free, unmask themselves or come to know Jesus as Savior and Lord.

I am thankful for my husband, Mark. Thank you for your display of "fruit" in our marriage. Your love and patience throughout this task have been precious. The moments we shared reading and chuckling at paragraphs in this book will forever be etched in my memory. Your comments about my choice of words in this book were invaluable, giving me a chuckle whenever I needed one. I appreciate your continual love and support, which have been highly beneficial in helping me complete this task.

I am thankful for the many women God has sent into my life to mold me, shape me and in some instances, gently and sternly correct me. That prepared me for this task. I am blessed because there are so many of you. The first woman is my mother, *Bernice.* What a woman of strength and wisdom and character! I appreciate her more now than ever as I still hear in my heart her words of wisdom, which I did not value when she spoke them. Mother, it was your voice that I heard over and over as I sometimes cried, sighed, giggled and laughed hilariously while completing these pages.

I am thankful for my siblings: Each of my four sisters, *Francine, Dene', Vernice and Rosele'*, has a special place in my heart because God has used her to supply a specific piece of clay to mold me into His woman. I call you my "sister-friends." My younger brother *Richard III,* serves as my "big brother": *Richard,* you have a heart of gold, giving me the care I need from a brother. To my youngest brother, the late Reganal, I miss you so much. Thank you all for the childhood memories that gifted me to pen this book.

I am thankful for my friend and mentor, *Mrs. Pamela Grant*: You pulled me out of my cocoon and helped me develop into a butterfly. I heard your voice so many times while penning this script. I still reminisce about that day, over 35 years ago, when I said yes to Jesus and how you held me in your arms as I wept in repentance. You shared with me the benefits I had received in my decision. Your love and wisdom helped me complete this task.

I am thankful for my long-time friend and prayer partner, *Ms. Yvette Breckenridge,* for taking me by the hand, leading me to the altar, and kneeling with me. You prayed for my heart when I could not. God used your prayers to position me to birth this book.

I am thankful for my friend, *Mrs. Madelyn Delancey.* God used you to read excerpts from my manuscript and give me constructive critique. Your critique helped me hear the thoughts I needed to hear, which opened up the floodgates, enabling me to complete this manuscript.

I am thankful for *Rev. Richard Watson*, my long-time friend and Sunday school co-teacher. You imparted fatherly wisdom to me when I needed the wisdom of an "earthly" father. Your words of wisdom, which rescued me so many times and helped me on my journey, are echoed in these pages.

Thank you, Mrs. Tonica Boyd. My gratitude for you is "threefold." The first reason, we share in our hearts. The second is your accepting the assignment to conduct my photoshoot and produce images for this work. You possess excellent photography skills at *JELSE Photography*. I am very pleased with your work. And third, thank you for your persistence in introducing me to your sister, the literary coach.

Deborah C. Anthony, my literary coach, thank you for "getting me." Each time I got stuck, with little effort, you got me back on track. Your love, compassion and patience for your clients is phenomenal. Our relationship has truly been a godsend as we are kindred spirits. You gave me the bigger picture from the start, and that helped me get to the finish line. Again, thank you!

Special thanks to my trainers at *KEEP FIT, Inc.* personal training studio, South Holland, Illinois and to my nutritionist and health coach at *The Fragrance House*, Harvey, Illinois (www.HowUEat.com). God used you both to get me to a place of wellness, on my journey to wholeness.

ENDORSEMENTS

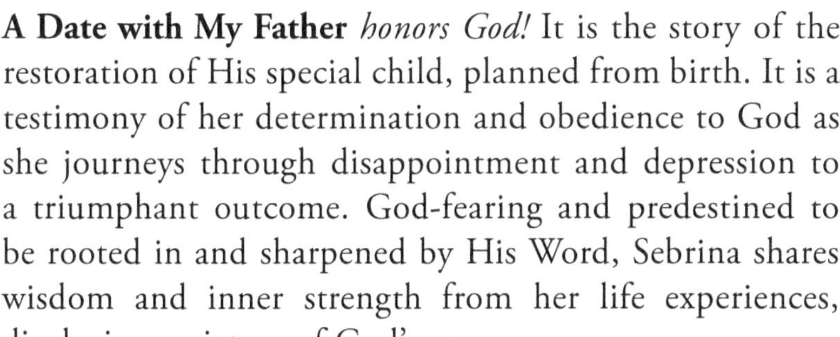

A Date with My Father *honors God!* It is the story of the restoration of His special child, planned from birth. It is a testimony of her determination and obedience to God as she journeys through disappointment and depression to a triumphant outcome. God-fearing and predestined to be rooted in and sharpened by His Word, Sebrina shares wisdom and inner strength from her life experiences, displaying a picture of God's grace.

Dene Jackson

You will experience so many emotions while reading **A Date with My Father**. What a transformation! Sebrina shows us God is everything. We can do all things through Him if we only turn our lives over to him. You too can be transformed: "*Blessed are all who fear the LORD, who walk in obedience to Him*" (Psalm 128:1).

Vernice Veal

The introduction grabs you from the beginning. I have known Sebrina for over 40 years. Our friendship began not long after we met. This book is a transparent view of God's will for her life. "**A Date with My Father**" can be a teaching tool, showing you God's ability to sustain you. Sebrina is still dating her "Father."

Althia Pamela Grant

FOREWORD

Rev. Yvette Breckenridge

There are some quotes, some literary giants that seem to know how to convey the things we feel deeply as humans. First, Helen Keller said, "What we have once enjoyed deeply we can never lose. All that we love deeply becomes a part of us." She seemed to grasp the depths of the feelings many of us experience in the darkness of loss and grief. This darkness can take us to difficult places. However, during our lifetimes, Christian transformation often allows us to reflect on the insides of lives that need work and, within them, Christ's redeeming power. Although the psychologist, Ram Dass, may have been considering another higher authority when he wrote this statement, it is still appropriate: "Our whole spiritual transformation brings us to the point where we realize that in our own being, we are enough." Although self-reliance might have contributed to Dass's statement, Christian self-realization comes through the Holy Spirit and revelation to help us discover in our lives with Christ that we are more than enough (Romans 8:31-39).

In my over 30 years of knowing this author as a Christian single woman, a married woman, a mother to many, a counselor, a teacher, and a friend, she has been credible and godly.

This book will help readers journey through a chronicle of self-discovery. It will enable them to learn self-restraint and become more reflective about accepting themselves despite hostility and struggle. Every person encounters many of these challenges. The writer also speaks of the unique experiences military families face in their sacrifices for this country. The author helps readers peer into the stressors military families face and the impacts on their children, and generally shows us strength and tenacity and confusion and fear.

Whether single, married, widowed, or divorced, we can all understand the encounters we have with others who love us as occurring through various life phases, including disappointments and sickness. However, the author provides insight into what happens when we feel we are not enough, especially for ourselves. She offers readers a chance to unmask and look at the areas of our lives in which we may need transformation.

A Date with My Father provides a road map that we Christians all need in our lives to "let go of the hurt" and journey to "wholeness." Readers of this book can believe wholeheartedly in the biblical principles found in it after the transformation their lives take them through: As has been written, "Eye has not seen, nor ear heard, Nor have entered into the heart of man The things which God has prepared for those who love Him" (1 Corinthians 2:9 NKJ).

Rev. Yvette Breckenridge M.Div., M.A.
Director of Pastoral Care
Salem Baptist Church of Chicago
10909 S. Cottage Grove
Chicago, Illinois 60628

Table of Contents

INTRODUCTION

I have heard a statement said in so many ways: "God makes all the plans for us in life and does not feel the need to check in with us," or "We plan, and God laughs," or "We make plans; God makes decisions." I can identify with each statement because I am naturally a planner. I cannot explain why. All I know is that God wired me that way. I plan and organize just about everything. Note that I did not say I "planned" everything.

This book will walk you through my formative experiences, meandering around my attaining age 18 and eventually settling into my later adult years. From those years, I share many life lessons I have learned along the way. The lessons learned affected not only my life but also many other lives, including those of my husband, students, mentees, counselees, friends, and family members.

As a younger adult, I did not realize how systematic I was. Looking back, I did everything in some type of order. I continued into adulthood, governing my life in that same manner and, thus, planning everything. It was planted in my heart at a very young age that I would continue my education beyond high school, so I immediately began planning my exodus from high school to university. I also knew that

I needed to make many adult decisions concerning my spiritual life and my post-educational life that would take me to a career and family. As I previously mentioned, I believe we make plans and God laughs. While I was trying to figure everything out, God already had a blueprint designed just for me. Everything had already been planned: my education and the avenues I'd take as I journeyed toward marriage, soothing me through a quest to bear a child that would end in barrenness. The struggles I would face on my journey through adulthood and that would eventually drive me through states of denial and disappointment before bringing me to depression were not a surprise to Him.

I share my journey with you for information and for transformation. I hope that you will identify with my journey through the words I communicate on the pages that follow, that these words may free you or even save you from unintended solitude.

Chapter 1
Growing Up

For as long as I can remember, I have been an analytical thinker. I ponder everything. I believe this character trait was born out of hearing my father say, "Sebrina, everything that comes up does not have to come out of your mouth. Think about what you are saying." This statement set me on the path to stopping and thinking before I spoke. Sometimes it worked against me, causing me to mull over things that did not really matter. My father challenged me often, so I was always looking for the next challenge.

As I grew through childhood and into an adult, I learned to respect him as an authority on everything. There was nothing I did not think my father knew. In retrospect, I revered him since I did not have a relationship with God, the Father. I feared my father just enough to keep me in line. If Daddy said it, it was the law in my mind. I remember that, when I was five, I was the only black child in my kindergarten class. Because I grew up living predominately among other races and I was always the one child who represented the black race in my circles, this was not an abnormal experience. One day, as we were coloring in my kindergarten class, one of my classmates blurted out, "My mommy says you are black!"

I quickly explained, "No, I am brown."

She yelled angrily, "My mommy said you are black!"

I yelled even louder that I was brown. I took a black crayon and a brown crayon, scribbled with each color, and compared my skin to both. She would not back down and continued to yell that I was black until the teacher sent us to opposite corners of the classroom. That evening, I told Daddy what that little girl had said to me. I was so surprised when he took her side and said, "Sebrina, you are black."

In tears, I dropped my head, saying, "No, Daddy. I am brown."

He picked me up in his arms, consoled me, and explained the difference between race and color. I thought about what I would say to my classmate. The next day, I simply explained to her, "My daddy says I am black with brown skin, and my blood is red just like yours."

I became a confident little girl because my daddy said that, although I was different, I was the same, and I belonged in that classroom along with the other kids. Whenever anybody said anything to me that did not make sense, once I had thought about it, I had to run it by my daddy. Daddy did not always flat out give me the answer. He made me think about it. Many times, my thoughts got the best of me as I would ponder the same thing over and over.

My father had a career in the United States Air Force, so I grew up military. As a result, my siblings and I were referred to as "military brats." We were mostly born in different states, and one of the younger ones was born outside the States, in Japan. I was born in North Carolina. Other than what I have read, I know nothing about it as I lived there for less than one year after my birth. As a young child, living in various states was exciting. As I went from one school to another, I had no problem being the "new" kid. Then I reached my teens, at which point it became difficult to fit in as the new kid. Daddy was very stern, strict, and protective. He expected excellence, and I mistook it for perfection. I believe that was when I developed my A-type personality: Everything always had to be neat and orderly.

Daddy had Papa Bear syndrome: "These are my cubs. Don't touch." He treated us all special, giving each of us the necessary attention based on our individual personalities.

Being military brats, we were exposed to many different cultures as we traveled and lived in many different places. Daddy was stationed in Dover, Delaware, when I was around 6. I remember him buying us a set of encyclopedias. The set contained 21 volumes, encompassing subjects classified under letters A through Z with an additional six volumes that were storybooks, perfect for family reading and bedtime stories. My mother and father read to us a lot and encouraged us to read daily. I learned a lot from reading those volumes as they were my "go to" when I needed help understanding and completing my homework assignments. They were also a solution for boredom.

It was not unusual for my siblings and I to gather around the dining room table, each child with his/her own volume, leaping through discussions of different stories and illustrations. Those encyclopedias served as our family home computer, which housed the "internet." Because watching television in our home was a privilege and not a right, we used the volumes for entertainment whenever we were restricted to inside play as the climate was cold and not always conducive to outside play. I became a very sociable kid because, growing up with six other siblings, there was always lots of interaction. This environment forced me to be an extrovert, but I really preferred being an introvert. I enjoyed my alone time, and reading provided that atmosphere. Reading took me away, so I developed a love for it, and I read anything that allowed me to get away.

I do not have memories of reading the Bible daily, and I did not grow up in the church. Although my family did not attend church regularly, its teachings were instilled in us. My parents raised us with Christian values as they used the principles of the Bible as their guide. Once we became old enough, each of us was given a scripture from the Bible to memorize. The youngest was always assigned *"Jesus wept"* (John 11:35). My scripture was *"Thou shalt have no other gods before Me"* (Exodus 20:3). Daddy explained that nothing or nobody should take the place of God in my life. I did not understand it, but I accepted it because he said it.

I remember us sitting around the dining room table at mealtimes, reciting our Bible verses one by one, then holding hands as Daddy said the blessing over our food. This was only one example of Biblical instruction we received. I remember being out with the family another time and Daddy explaining to us that, when crossing the street, we should only cross from corner to corner. He said crossing the street from side to side in the middle of the block was dangerous; drivers were more likely to see us if we stood at a corner and to yield us the right of way. This was one of many lessons Daddy taught us while we were growing up that I now recall as a life lesson. Once he taught us a lesson, he expected us to learn from it and use it.

One day, I was walking home from a friend's home, three blocks away. After passing the corner, I decided to cross the street anyway. I was midway across when I heard a horn blow and my name called. It was Daddy. I ran to the car and grabbed the handle to get in, only to be denied entry. Daddy said, "Come here." Excited to see Daddy, I skipped around to the driver's side, only to hear, "Sebrina, what did I teach you about crossing streets?" After I regurgitated his instructions, he directed me to go back to the corner and cross the street correctly. He pulled off, leaving me to walk the remaining block home, and waited for me in the driveway.

I repeated his instructions to myself all the way down the block, wishing I had followed them. I was so hurt that I had disappointed him. He kneeled so that he was at my eye level and said, "When I tell you to do something, I expect you to do it whether I am watching you or not." Today, I almost always cross the street from corner to corner, but when faced with the decision to cross a street from the middle of the block instead of from corner to corner, I have difficulty crossing it. That lesson was a character builder in the department of integrity. It taught me to always do the right thing whether someone was looking or not.

When I was turning 12, we moved from Delaware to Louisiana. As we did in most relocations, we initially moved to the Military Base housing. We lived in Bossier City at the Barksdale Air Force Base (Shreveport was the city next door). It was summer, so I had a few weeks before school started. Having that time was good since my anxiety levels were building as I anticipated my first day at my new school. One comforting thing about going to new schools as I was growing up was that I always had a sibling who went to school with me. This time, there were a high school, a middle school, and an elementary school in the mix. I was the middle child, and it was my turn to go to middle school all alone. The older girls went to the high school, and the younger went to the elementary school. My middle school was a sixth-through-eighth-grade school. I was in the sixth grade, my older sisters were in grades nine through 11, and the younger ones were in the first, fourth, and fifth grades. I really felt out of place.

As soon as we got settled in our new home, Daddy had to leave for Guam for a one-year tour of duty. He was not home to take me to school for my first day as he usually would. Mother did not drive, so the school bus was my only option. That was the first time in my life that going to school was a scary experience. I remember that, after the first day of school, we sat at the dinner table. That evening, my siblings talked about their day, sharing its highlights and finishing each other's sentences. I remained silent, feeling like I could not compete as I did not have a partner to help me report my day. I remember this being the beginning of my disassociating myself from my siblings and becoming a true introvert. My older sisters would go shopping together, and the younger would go down the street to play in the park, while I would stay in my room reading.

I was always interacting with a book. My mother would suggest to me several times during the day that I go outside and get some fresh air. I would beg her to let me retreat to my fairy tale in my book. There were times when Mother insisted that I come to sit with her, pulling me away from my book to have me engage with the "real world." I remember sitting alone with her, void of competition from my siblings and feeling very comforted. Normally, Mom did not share her Coke Cola with us, but, during these times, she shared it with me. Since we were not allowed to drink Mom's Coke Cola, this was a treat. During that year of Daddy's absence, my alone time with Mom became a regular activity. I divided my time between talking with Mom and spending time in my personal space. Since there were more of us than rooms, our personal space was marked by a chair between our beds in a bedroom for two or three. My bed became my premium space because no one ever occupied it but me. It became my place of security, comfort, and solitude.

A year passed, and Daddy came home from Guam. He decided to retire after 20 years of service in the United States Air Force. Upon his retirement, we moved to Shreveport, Louisiana, the city just outside Bossier City, and began living the civilian life. I went to a new school called Lakeshore Junior High School. It also consisted of three grades, but it started with the seventh grade and ended with the ninth. When we were midway through the eighth grade, parents, along with the teachers, decided whether children would move to the high school or complete the ninth grade at the junior high school level. I remember being torn about whether to stay at the junior high school or go on to the senior high school. That was mainly because, in my two years at Lakeshore, I had become very close to two girls in band class, Deb and Cyndi. In the end, Deb and I influenced our parents' decision to have us go on to the senior high school, but we still ended up attending different schools.

During my second year of attending high school, when I was 15, our parents decided to move from Shreveport, Louisiana, to Chicago, Illinois. The move was a result of Daddy's decision not to reenlist in the Air Force for another

20-year tour. His primary reason for retiring after 20 years was his feeling that he had already missed some of the most prominent years of our upbringing. His retirement just came too soon for me, making this move an unhappy transfer.

I felt like I was coming into my own, finishing my first two years of high school and having just the right combination of teachers and friends. I played first chair in the marching band, and everybody knew me as the "female" trumpet player. I was going to be a "big time" upperclassman, leading the brass section of the Fair Park High School marching band. I was on target to receive a music scholarship to the popular historic black college, Gambling State University. When the news came that we were moving, my heart sank, and many questions began to flood my mind. Where would I finish high school? What about my friends? Would I be accepted in band? Who would take me to prom? Would my new school acknowledge my "perfect" high school attendance record? Where would I attend college? There were so many uncertainties that I needed a plan to calm my heart.

So, I made a pact with my friend Deb, whom I had met in the seventh grade at Lakeshore Junior High School in Shreveport. We had actually met in band class, where we played in the brass section of the band together. Then we had become playmates and would spend time together after school and on weekends at each other's homes. After being separated to attend different high schools, and now facing an even more permanent separation, we made a pact that we would attend college in Texas together upon our graduation from high school.

When I arrived in Chicago with my family, it was the same scenario as when we had arrived in Shreveport. We arrived in the summertime, so I had a few weeks to anticipate my first day of school. That summer, turning 16 allowed me to qualify for a work permit, so my cousin introduced me to his boss, and I began working as a clerical employee. Having this job helped a lot. It gave me focus and helped soothe my anxieties as I anticipated continuing high school in the fall.

Following that summer, I enrolled in the Dr. Martin Luther King High School as a junior. I was able to keep my summer job, so I choose a schedule that allowed me to take required courses during the morning sessions. As I had done at my previous high school, I excelled in all my classes. I maintained a favorable grade point average and perfect attendance. However, I did not enroll in the band. Working at the Credit Bureau as a clerical employee was very fulfilling. I did not feel the need to get involved at school. Mom disagreed. She thought I needed some extracurricular activity because all I did was go to school, work, and study. I had no outside activities. At my mother's suggestion, I got involved in one club.

Mom was pleased as she explained she wanted my high school experience to be memorable, but all I wanted was to get finished and close that chapter. The club I choose was the "Queens of King." This club was very structured and had extremely strict requirements. It was a low-maintenance club that would help me meeting my goal of just getting through high school and starting my next chapter. The club targeted girls who were upperclassmen, had a 95% attendance record, were college-bound, and had an above-average grade point average. The purpose of the club was to assist upperclassmen in their preparation for college and careers. Ms. Bouie, a black female teacher, was a great example as she coordinated the group. She was incredibly sophisticated and savvy, and she pushed us to be similar. I participated in many activities the club offered as well as many senior activities, including the spring dance, senior luncheon, prom, and senior trip. I continued working my job part-time for three hours after school and five hours on Saturdays until I graduated. Working full-time during the summer was great preparation for college. It gave me needed social and academic skills, not to mention yielding me a hefty bank account that supplemented my scholarships, and grants.

Dawning Adulthood

I grew up as one of seven children. I had three older sisters, one younger sister (my Irish twin), and two younger brothers. Yes, I was smack-dab in the middle with middle-child syndrome. Most times, I did not fit with the older or younger since there was an almost-two-year difference between me and the youngest of my older sisters, and I just did not fit in with my younger siblings.

I was more mature than the younger ones, who were referred to as the "babies." In no way did I fit that description. Mother and Grandmother described me another way. They referred to me as "the one that has been here before." Not only was I the middle child, but I was also the special child of the seven as I was born on the seventh day of the seventh month at 7:17 am. At my arrival, the doctor announced to my parents, "This child is going to be lucky with all these sevens." Because of my position in birth, I had middle-child syndrome, which made me question where I fit in. I felt like

I needed to grow up fast, so I blew through my childhood as I replaced playtime with analysis time. I was always so serious and trying to figure out my next step. Although it was not my responsibility to figure things out in my younger years, I found myself always looking ahead and planning how I could take my next step.

As I approached age 18, my excitement about going to Houston was at an all-time high: Deb and I had kept our pact. We had submitted our applications to three universities in Texas with the promise that we would attend the university where we both got accepted. We chose the University of Houston, and my most exciting anticipation was executing my plan to transition from Chicago to Houston. The decision to continue my education right after high school was not optional. It had always been the plan, but the location was purely my decision. I had started the process of making this decision well in advance because, after Deb and I had made our pact, that was all I had been able to think about. Thinking about going to school in Texas after graduation had helped to ease the pain of the unexpected transfer and living in Chicago. I had moved from state to state all my life with no input as to where we would go next. This time, the decision was mine. The decision to go to school in Texas was the most important decision of my life (so I thought). I had tunnel vision as I planned every detail surrounding my life after high school and making my exodus from Chicago.

Saying Goodbye to Daddy

In preparation for my exodus from Chicago, Daddy said he wanted us to spend one-on-one time together one afternoon before I left for school. I remember being excited at the thought of just him and me spending a whole afternoon together. He explained, "There are some things Daddy wants to talk to you about before you leave to start your journey to becoming a responsible adult." I believe Daddy realized that, by sheltering me, he had painted rosy pictures of life in the world and wanted to open my eyes to a few things before I left for school. We planned our date a few weeks after my 18th birthday that July.

The Saturday before our date, I got a call while at work: Daddy had been rushed to the hospital. When I arrived, he was unresponsive. The clinicians told me the ventilator was breathing for him, allowing him to rest. They explained that he could still hear me and invited me to sit close and talk to him. As soon I touched Daddy's body, I knew that he had made his transition. His flesh lay in that bed, but his heart was gone. My heart sank as I realized I would miss my date with my daddy in the coming week and would not ever get to reschedule it.

Remembering our many conversations, I realized why Daddy had wanted to spend time with me before I left for school. I finished high school at 17 with lots of head knowledge but very immature. I was on my way to school young, tender-hearted, sheltered, and inexperienced in facing the world. I believe he wanted to make sure I was prepared for the wolves. Daddy and I did not get a chance to have our talk. However, the Lord prepared me with wisdom and knowledge that kept me from the kinds of experiences I believe he had feared.

Months leading up to my departure for school, I developed a relationship with a young man who was what I call "my first Romans 8:28 experience without knowing anything about

Romans 8:28." Robert and I met through a mutual friend. He became my prom date and remained in my life for the next *five* years. He was five years older than me and more mature than me but was not fully mature for his age. Let us just say he was at the right maturity level for me. As you can imagine, I left home with a broken heart that was filled with many unanswered questions, *making me very vulnerable as a young girl away from home and alone for the first time.* Robert became my covering as I committed to him and considered myself off limits to the males at school. As a result, I did not entertain any relationships while away at school that year. If I was not in class, studying, sleeping, or hanging out with my roommate or floormates, I was talking to Robert on the telephone or writing him a letter. He helped me get through some of the hard times associated with missing home and particularly Daddy.

That is why, in hindsight, I call this relationship experience "my first Romans 8:28 experience." Many Christians and non-Christians alike use this scripture out of context. They quote it as *"All things work together for the good."* But, according to the Bible, Romans 8:28 states, ***"And we know*** *that* ***all*** *things work together for the good* ***to*** *them* ***that*** *love God, to them who are the* ***called*** *according to His purpose."* Since this scripture begins with a conjunction, we must consider the previous verse because the word "and" connects it to the previous verse, which explains how God makes intercessions for the *saints.* This verse works as the qualifier regarding who may claim this promise. I had not put my hope in Christ at this point in my life, so I could not rightfully claim it. Therefore, I call my experience a Romans 8:28 experience, because I did not know the Lord was working on my behalf to turn my bad situation around for a long-term good. I knew God but did not have a relationship with Him. Having this relationship with Robert protected me in my innocence. He acted as a covering for me since Daddy was no longer there, and I had not connected with my Heavenly Father. I was fair game because I was so naïve. Other than going on dates with Robert after prom, I had no experience dating and spending time with young men. I believe having my preparation date with Daddy before going off to school would have defused some if not all that naivety.

Leaving for School

Daddy remained in a coma for an additional five days after I saw him; I limply prepared my belongings, scheduled to leave for school the following week. Mother said I should go on to school. She believed Daddy would recover and be there when I returned home. I felt differently, but I obeyed her and commenced to pack so that I could leave the following week. My flight was put on hold two days prior to my leaving when the ventilator was removed and daddy flatlined. Regret flooded my heart as, when I'd had the opportunity, I had not sat at Daddy's bedside and said all the things I had planned to say on our date. I hadn't talked to him because, in my heart, I'd hoped we would still have an opportunity to talk once he regained consciousness.

Taking no time to grieve my loss, a week later, I flew to Houston. I arrived at the university numb and disoriented. I had missed everything: freshman orientation, which included registration for freshman-level classes; the dormitory orientation; campus tours; and my interview for my work-study job. The next three months, I felt like I was having an out-of-body experience. I sat in lectures but did not comprehend them. I read lessons but could not concentrate or recall what I'd read. I slept every opportunity I got. When the semester ended, I was placed on academic probation. Subsequently, I packed my belongings and returned home. Once I returned home, I grieved the loss of my daddy as I thought of him daily. Missing my daddy, and now back at home, I was broken and lost. I felt empty and defeated. With no backup plan, I was not sure what to do next.

What Do I Do Now?

Every day, the question "What do I do now?" echoed in my head. After two months of downtime, my mother answered my question without me asking. She lovingly said, "Sebrina, either enroll in school or find a job."

I was out of sorts because this was not the plan. Still, the question rang through my mind: "What do I do now?"

I did not have a plan for myself, but the Lord had a plan. One day, Mother woke me up and told me to get dressed to accompany her to the Social Security office to respond to a letter she had received. In the office, I observed folders piled three and four high at each representative's desk. Some piles continued onto the floor alongside their desks. There were trays of paper everywhere. As I sat there pondering, I asked the representative, "Why is this office so messy?"

He replied, "We don't have enough workers! Do you need a job?"

Before I could answer, my mother said, "Yes, she does!"

I completed a job application, took a typing test, and interviewed with the manager all while my mother was conducting her business. The Lord even planted a reference in the office for me. The boss's secretary was one of my colleagues from my high school graduating class and a member of my high school club, the Queens of King. We'd both graduated in the top 10% of our class, and we'd shared several classes in our senior year, so she knew me well enough to give a reference, and her boss gladly accepted her recommendation to hire me. The next week, I received a job offer. Anybody that really knows me has heard my story about my interviewing for my first *real* job in jeans, sneakers, and my University of Houston sports jersey with my mother sitting next to me. This is what I call a "God thing." It is something that I describe with the words "Nobody but God can do a thing like that!"

Chapter 2
Adult Decisions

Leaving School Behind

Growing up, I heard the expression "Hindsight is 20/20," over and over. I did not pay it much attention until I became an adult. Then I echoed the expression because, looking back, the first decisions I made as an adult were good decisions but just not in the right order. One important decision I made as an adult, was accepting my first job offer as a clerical employee with the Social Security Administration (SSA). In retrospect, it was a God decision. Upon returning home, my self-esteem had been irreparably damaged by the academic probation mark on my academic record after I'd graduated at the top of my high school class. This job offer was just what I needed to restore my impaired self-esteem, especially after returning home and needing to get a job, buy a car, and rent an apartment, all in one year.

The position was a temporary one. I was hired on a "not to exceed 700 hours" appointment. It had been designed as a summer job. This type of appointment worked for me because it gave me time to think about the answer to my question, "What do I do now?" If you do the math, that was about nine paychecks. They would have provided enough money for me to enroll in school, buy books and clothes, and contribute to Mom's household expenses. That might have sounded like a good plan, but it was not for me. I decided to save towards moving into my own apartment after accepting an extension of my appointment, which subsequently became a permanent career position.

I have shared this story with many people through the years. Those without hope and faith, just said, "You were lucky."

Others said, "You were in the right place at the right time."

I disagree; I believe it was God-ordained. God set me on a course on the day when I visited the Social Security office with my mother. In hindsight, my good decision on that day was really a God decision. As I can see now, many decisions in my life were not good decisions but God decisions. The doctor that delivered me did not have the right perspective on my being born on July 7 at 7:17am. He should have presented me to my parents, saying, "Here is your special child." I believe God has always had a special hand on me, gently pushing me into place, pulling me back at other times, and carrying me at others.

When I accepted the offer to work for the Social Security Administration (SSA), I was not planning to return to school in the fall. I was still in the "What do I do now?" phase. My mother wanted to make sure I structured my life such that I'd be able to take care of myself and finish school. She approved of my accepting the job but took every opportunity to remind me of the importance of enrolling in school the next semester. Once I became a "career" employee, however, opportunities for me to advance to the next pay-grade level opened. I quit school again and continued pursuing my career with SSA. Although this was a great opportunity and a wise decision to pursue, in hindsight, quitting school was not a wise decision. It had *not* been God's will that I go away and make a mess of school, but His grace and mercy had prevailed. As a result of my full-time permanent position, I was soon renting an apartment on my own, purchased a car, and returned to school part-time. I was 19, living alone in my apartment, which I had fully furnished on my own, and feeling accomplished despite my failed degree attempt. Today, I tell young people, "Go to school first!" I had a great career with SSA. God's grace and mercy continued to prevail throughout my career. I had no degree, yet He blessed me with a respectable professional career. I did not have a bachelor's degree for 34 years of my career. What I did have was a degree of the Master. The "Master" took me to places of achievement that only He could take credit for. Again, it was a "*God* thing!"

Embracing My Career Path

My temporary position, which I expected not to exceed 700 hours, became a lifelong career of 36 years. During this period, I was promoted 10 times. What I call "God decisions" prevailed throughout my career. After my 700-hour appointment was extended, I got another "not to exceed" appointment of two years. During that two-year appointment, a permanent position became available and I was not only promoted to it but also to the next grade level. In this position, I served as a clerical employee under two Social Insurance Representatives. One was younger and straight out of college, and the other was an older woman in her 50s. Her name was Ms. Minnie; she became my mother hen. Remember, I was young, sheltered, and inexperienced. She took me under her wing and taught me the job and some life lessons about conducting myself in the workplace. She was very neat and organized in a junky office, so I learned to organize my work meticulously by watching her. She taught me when to speak up and when to remain silent. She dressed professionally, even on dress-down Friday, and so did I. She came to work rain or shine, so I came to work rain or shine. You get it: She taught me work ethics.

One day, Ms. Minnie asked, "Sebrina, what are you doing?"

I replied, "Updating our work tally."

She asked, "Do you plan to do this for the rest of your career?" She further explained, "You have a lot of potential to be promoted to the next level. I suggest you apply for one of these next-level permanent career postings." Then she went on to explain how I needed to complete the application by the filing deadline. It seemed easy enough, so I took Ms. Minnie's advice and applied for three of the six job postings that interested me. Two weeks later, I got called for an interview that yielded a job offer. I accepted the offer and was scheduled to start my new position in two weeks when I got another job offer for a higher pay rate. I rescinded my first job acceptance and accepted the new offer since it had promotion potential. Ms. Minnie explained that I should accept that position because it would set me on a better career path, especially once I finished school. Accepting the promotion put me in another income bracket, which disqualified me for my school financial aid. My pending student loans were already overwhelming, so I decided not to continue school until I could pay for my classes upon registering. In hindsight, I wish I had sought wise counsel before making the decision to put school on hold. But Ms. Minnie was right about accepting that promotion setting me on a better career path. It was God's mercy prevailing again because, despite my failure to finish school, the promotions continued to come one after another.

Chapter 3

Meeting My Heavenly Father

I was on the fast track in my career and still experiencing Romans 8:28 moments without really knowing the meaning of Romans 8:28. I thought I was just missing Daddy, but, in hindsight, I was missing my Father, my Savior, whom I so desperately needed. As I continued to seek fulfillment, I was invited to a church service by a woman I met at a Tupperware party. I declined the invitation, thinking I needed more time to ponder this idea of going to church. Although I was not moving rapidly towards making plans to attend church regularly, I could not get the thought out of my mind. I believe the Lord used the Tupperware lady to revive the seed that had been planted in my heart years before. Weeks later, I reconnected with a high school friend who attended church regularly. She invited me to attend a special church service, and I attended service with her for the next six weeks.

That was not my first experience attending church. My first memory of going to church was in Dover, Delaware, when I was eight years old. That summer, we went to Sunday school every Sunday. A yellow school bus would pick my siblings and I up and take us to church for an hour. We got dressed up in our school clothes and took our pencils and New Testament Bibles every week. I remember singing catchy songs about Jesus and the ice cream bar we received each week when we returned home and exited the bus.

The next time I experienced church was in Shreveport, Louisiana, at 12. My sisters and I got invited to church by our neighborhood playmates. We went to church with them for a few Sundays and asked our parents if we could join because we wanted to sing in the choir like them. Once we joined, I recall the pastor asking me, "Where do you want to work in the church, young lady?" I said I wanted to work in the choir because singling in the choir seemed like fun rather than work. I did not fully understand the salvation story before my baptism, so I did not receive Christ in my heart before getting baptized. The next Sunday we all got baptized. I call this my *watering* experience because God sent me to that Church as a teen to *plant* a desire for Christ in my heart, and later, when I received Christ, he presented me as an addition to the body of Christ (1 Corinthians 3:7).

I attended church for six weeks. On the seventh Sunday, as on the six previous Sundays, I called my friend to let her know I was leaving my home to pick her up for church, only to hear that she would not be going. Staying home was not an option; I was not ready to end my search for fulfillment. The Lord put it in my heart to call Joyce, my new "Tupperware lady" friend, whose invitation to attend her church I had previously declined. That Sunday, I met Jesus and accepted Him as Lord and Savior (He was my Savior right away, I learned to allow Him to be Lord soon after). He emptied me out that day and filled me with His precious Holy Spirit, and my real life began. My decision to go to church on that day was not a "good decision" but a "God decision." As I got to know Christ, I began to understand all the things working together for good in my life (Romans 8:28).

Teaching Moments

As I read and studied the Bible and sought His face in prayer, God allowed me to move to the next level in Christian growth. He led me to many resources to help me learn His Word. I walked through every open door into opportunities that included other church services, conferences, Bible classes, self-help books, online studies, and spiritual retreats. I spent the next three years drenching my heart, mind, and soul with the Word.

The excitement I'd had when preparing to go to college overflowed in my heart again. I woke up every day wondering what the Lord would bring on that day, what instructions He would give me, and where He would take me. I desired the sincere milk of the Word and fed on it daily (1 Peter 2:2). As I grew in His word, I went from feeding on milk to feasting on the meat of the Word. As the Bible says, *"To whom much is given, much is required"* (Luke 12:48). The closer I got to God, the more challenges I faced. It became difficult to stay focused, and my first instinct was to slow down, but whenever I turned away from the Word, I felt broken again. Not wanting to ever experience disconnection from the Lord, I quickly ran back to the Word. It became my hiding place. The Word was my secret place, a place I could retreat to for warmth; it was like wrapping myself in a warm blanket on a cold wintery day.

One of the greatest challenges I faced as a young adult Christian was my health. I was already sick when I got saved, but I did not know the extent of my illness. The Lord directed me to seek Him concerning my health. Because I am a seeker by nature, my first response when I need to know something is to study. In seeking resources that could help me learn more about holistic healing, I found a class at the local junior college. I decided to enroll in the holistic healing class taught by the author, Queen Afua. Her book was titled "Heal Thyself," and she taught it in a six-week course. It was just what I needed as it helped me to understand my physical and spiritual body and gave me a sense of self. The information was phenomenal. I was so excited that I wanted to jump right in without stopping to commit my way to the Lord and asking Him for direction.

The next week I started a 10-day water fast without any preparation. I accomplished it by the grace of God because this type of fasting is very difficult if one is not walking in the presence of the Lord. The purpose of my fast was to cleanse my body and awaken my spiritual awareness. The problem was that I did not take my newfound knowledge seriously. I was supposed to use this knowledge to start a new lifestyle of healthy eating since my bad food choices were the culprit where my health issues were concerned. I did not follow through. Instead, I cleaned up my eating just enough to get a short-term fix. Shortly after celebrating a positive result, I fell back into my old ways. My experience was like the description in Romans 6, which taught me that anything dead could no longer rule me. I did not put my old ways to death; I just put them to sleep. Had I put them to death, I would have accomplished my goal of overcoming my health issue in that season of my life.

My biggest problem was my excess weight, which led to obesity then to an array of other diagnoses. My doctors suggested early on that I should lose weight. Losing it was not the problem; I just struggled to keep it off. Because I had built faith in the Word, I thought that, with God, all things were possible and, this time, I would lose it with God's help and keep it off. It was still a struggle because I did not face the *real* issues behind my weight gain. It was easier to just pull the drape over them and pretend they were not there. In my world, while being overweight was frowned upon, it was acceptable. I was always soothed by being told that, instead of worrying I should do something about it and would do it when I was ready. But I never could seem to get ready. There was always something more pressing to deal with that demanded my time and attention. Especially since food was my comforter, companion, and stress reliever. When I disciplined my life to transition into the Christian life, I left that area out of the transition.

During this time in my life, the Lord took me to John 15:7, which suggested to me that He would not withhold my request if I walked in obedience to Him. This was an "if–then" statement: "If you do this, I will do that," says the Lord. I did not receive my request for a healed body because I did not surrender the bad eating. God is not man; He does not lie, He does exactly what He says He will do the way He says He will do it (Numbers 23:19). He had no need to repent, but I did. I needed to turn around and go in a totally different direction. He even provided the road map by sending me to the holistic health class. Knowing that Romans 8:1 told me I was not condemned, I still walked in secret condemnation provoked by my excessive weight. I wanted to go full speed ahead, but the image I saw in the mirror was not the one I saw in my head. The reflection in the mirror was my biggest enemy. That reflection robbed me of my self-esteem as dwelling on it paralyzed me in my very being, preventing me from moving forward with the things God was literally handing me. All around me were resources to help me overcome my hurts, habits, and hang-ups, which would free me, leading me to a successful weight loss journey.

My highest weight was 272 pounds as I moved into my late 40s. It was ironic because, for my 40th birthday, I bought a health club membership at the Experience Fitness club just five miles from my home (another God thing). I was determined after reading an article that said the first step in weight loss was to get moving. I made up my mind that I was going to work out at least two times a week to get started. My life started in a new direction, but, once again, I lost my momentum and could no longer keep up my workout. Not only was I unable to maintain the weight loss I had achieved while working out, but I also gained even more weight.

The Lord's plan for my visit to the SSA office on that day in August had been twofold. First, it had satisfied my need for a job, and, second, it had planted me in a vineyard where I could be discipled into the faith. The office was filled with His workers. Ms. Minnie was my first encounter. She showed me the Love of Christ by meeting needs I did not realize I had. Then there was Ms. Mira. She loved the Lord, her husband, her children, and her job in that order. She had such a beautiful spirit. She was the real-deal Christian woman. She invited me to an all-day Saturday retreat at her church. The emphasis was on Psalm 27. This tugged at my heartstrings because, months before I'd come to the Lord, He'd directed me to read that very psalm and it was still resonating in my heart. When I had sought peace, the

Lord had directed me to read Psalm 27 to show me I was in darkness and the reason for my sadness. All I remember after reading it was a sense of peace coming over me, and I began to want more of that peace as a constant. When I was at the retreat, He took me back to that day and showed me that I was no longer in darkness because He was now my light, my salvation, and my strength. God favored me even before I favored Him. On that day, I moved from being a convert to being a disciple, and I began to live my life for Christ.

If we were honest in telling our salvation stories, many of us would admit to accepting Christ with our minds, not our hearts. On the day I gave my heart to the Lord, I mulled over the decision to turn my life over to Him because I thought I was not ready to fully commit. It was that perfection thing again. I felt like I needed to get things in order. I thought about not having an appropriate wardrobe. If I committed to becoming a member, I needed to buy some new dresses and shoes, or so I thought. I remember saying to myself, "I am not ready, I have to wait until I get myself together."

At that moment, the minister said to the congregation, "The Lord said you cannot get yourself together, you need to come to Him just as you are." I jumped out of my seat and gave my hand to the pastor, but I gave my heart to the Lord. Giving my heart to the Lord on that day was the best adult decision I had ever made. I remember feeling so free. It was like a load had been lifted off my shoulders. I was so tired from trying to figure out my life that accepting Christ gave me relief. I cried for hours on that day, surrendering my life to the Lord, which brought me relief.

I believe I was created in Christ's likeness in fulfillment of His purpose on Earth. Jesus came to earth, lived among us, was crucified, buried, and resurrected then ascended to heaven for me. Once His purpose on Earth was fulfilled, He took His rightful place beside the Father with me in mind. According to Psalm 139:14, I am fearfully and wonderfully created in God's character, which means I was patterned after His likeness. I was created just like Him, only I live in a body with a soul and a spirit on earth. Unlike an animal, I was born in a body with a soul and a spirit. I was born separated from God. In my born-again experience, I received the spirit of God in the presence of the Holy Spirit, which connected me to God.

At birth, my *body* was subject to its five senses: sight, smell, hearing, taste, and touch. My *soul* was subject to imagination, conscience, memory, reason, and affection. My *spirit* was dead until I was introduced to Christ and chose to surrender my body and soul to Him. Only then was my *spirit* subject to faith, hope, reverence, prayer, and worship. The revelation of Christ only came to me through my *spirit* man according to 1 Corinthians 1:9-16. Since being awakened in Christ and experiencing a new birth, I can depend on God to give me instructions for living my life as he works in me according to His will and choices for me (Philippians 2:13).

When I accepted Christ, I desired to change in all areas of my life. Christ gave me His promise that He would be with me to help me as I made my decision to change. As I began my transition, my old man (the natural me) fought against my new man (the spiritual me), and I struggled to do right in the presence of evil (Romans 7:14-20). When I accepted Christ as an adult, I was conditioned by a life of sin.

I needed to retrain my mind and my body to cooperate with my new spirit. This was not an easy task because I was prone to self-gratification, which included abusing my body with unhealthy food choices and lack of an exercise routine.

Learning that my body was the temple of the Holy Spirit was shocking. It took some years before I yielded to the Holy Spirit with my body, so sickness took hold and I almost lost the battle. After finally yielding, I accepted God's plan for my physical body to exercise and eat properly in order to receive my healing. As I searched the scriptures, I was amazed at the many references in the Bible concerning God's design for my physical body. He made mention that movement of my body was intended to glorify Him in Colossians 3, that everything I did in my body should glorify Him. One would have thought that, since our bodies were representative of Him, we would automatically represent Him with them. Truthfully, I had to decide to yield. Once I made the decision to change, the Lord did not leave me to myself; He sent me a nutritionist and a personal trainer who helped me work His restoration plan for my body, which was now lined up with my spirit.

My new nutrition and fitness program helped me to understand the need to be healed and whole. This meant I had to work on my physical self and my spiritual self. Understanding that there are dimensions of wellness, I believe that I have accomplished wholeness as I can identify with every dimension of wellness. Because wholeness is a journey, I am always working on my spiritual, social, mental and physical well-being. I was in sin because I ignored God's instructions about my physical body, especially since my body was meant to house the Holy Spirit (1 Corinthians 6:19). My body, a broken-down shack, was not fit for me to live in, let alone the Holy Spirit. I became embarrassed in my body as I stood to teach. In my mind, my body displayed disobedience while I stood in front of people, teaching obedience (I was convicted as the Lord allowed me to see myself). He allowed me to see the statement I was making with my sick body as I stood to teach the Word of God. I learned from James 4:17 that, as a Christian, I was expected to do better once I learned better, so when I choose not to do better, my actions spoke louder than my voice. Though I was sick, the Holy Spirit allowed me to be effective in my teaching until I wasn't (as I accepted my dying state). But the Lord whispered to me and said, "Shall we continue in sin, that grace may abound?" and He answered, "Certainly not!" (Romans 6:1). I became immobilized, unable to teach any longer. That was the Lord nudging me again. The Lord was concerned about every area of my life, as he is with all his children, and he did not allow me to continue in sin. I cast my cares on him and continued to pray, believing. He guided me to make sure I fulfilled the plan and purpose he had for my life.

My lifelong purpose is to fulfill the plan God has predestined for me. His plan is for me to testify of His goodness by teaching and counseling using the Word of God. He has blessed me to by guiding me in researching and interpreting His Word. He guides me in advising individuals as they share their problems with me and allows me to relay what He says in His Word. God placed me in many positions to counsel people in His word. I would see people receiving healing and deliverance from my counsel, yet I was still plagued with my illnesses and hurts. It was simple; I was not accepting the Word for myself. I was not yielding to God working His Word in me. Once I realized I needed to yield, I began to receive healing for my own hurts.

Mostly, I desire to be an ambassador for Christ, explaining the love of Christ and the importance of each lost soul's surrendering of his will to Christ. I desire to be a mouthpiece that will ensure a person understands God's plan and purpose for his life. I would like my life to be an example that people will learn from; I do not want them to repeat my negative history in their lives.

As a woman of influence, I desire to live a life that is pleasing to God in pursuit of my calling to teach the Word of God to those He sends my way. God has blessed me with this desire and given me the tools and resources to perform it. I believe that, as the Word of God continues to sharpen me, I will fulfill God's purpose for me on Earth. My goal is to continue to submit to Christ in my body as an honest and compassionate learner of His Word. I am determined to constantly renew myself by focusing on becoming a healthier me.

I Surrender

In giving my heart to Christ on that seventh Sunday of my return to Church as an adult, I repented of my sins. Since repenting involved surrendering, it took some time to totally surrender my heart. I spent the following months emptying out my heart and allowing the Lord to totally move in. I cried for days. Looking back, my tears were the Lord's way of cleansing me while showing me myself. He showed me a weak young woman who was broken and unresponsive. Responding to Christ's beckoning gave me hope again. I was on the road to recovery from the brokenness I developed from being a fatherless young adult, failing at college, and losing my way in life. I was becoming whole again as the Lord led me through the deep treasures of His Word. Because of my love for reading "a God thing," I began to read the Word as my preferred script. I could not put it down; I took my Bible everywhere I went and used every available moment to read it. It was like I was that little girl again, retreating to my personal space to steal away in a book. He was preparing me to read His word back then, when He allowed me to fall in love with reading.

The Lord healed my heart quickly as I labored in the Book of Psalms, the book that led me to Him, particularly Psalm 27. But it was Psalm 51 that made me realize my need to totally depend on Christ in that it shone the flashlight on my humanism and helped me stop my sins from overtaking me and pulling me away from a perfect Savior. The Word showed me that I was *imperfect*, while Christ was perfect. This was eye-opening because of my perfectionism during my battle with brokenness, and I gained the ability to put things in perspective again.

When the Lord called me, He called me with purpose. He called me to teach His Word at the age of 24. During this time in my life, I lived alone. It was the best time of my life because I was free to surrender to the Lord with no distractions. As I read my Bible and spent time talking to the Lord for many hours in the day and night, the Lord allowed me to fall in love with Him through His Word. For the first time, I was connected to God in his Word. I remember studying my Sunday school lesson all week long. I had my lesson outlined, the questions answered, and the weekly memory verse memorized every week, eager to participate in the lesson. I was so excited and felt privileged to be in Sunday school each week. One Sunday, my Pastor preached a sermon titled “Walking in your Purpose.” I had never thought of my life as having a purpose. I was working every day, taking care of myself. I was attending church every Sunday and regarded my ministry as singing in the choir. I also attended Wednesday night Bible class, and that was my life aside from dating Robert and hoping for a marriage proposal to start a family that I thought would make my life complete.

As I meditated on that sermon all week, the Lord finally said to me, “No one can serve two masters.” I heard it, but I did not comprehend it. The Holy Spirit brought it back to my spirit many times that week until I sat down and searched the scriptures for understanding. Thank God for my Thompson-chained reference Bible. There it was in Matthew 6:24, as clear as day. The Lord explained to me on that day that my devotion could not be split between Him and Robert because I could only be devoted to one while despising the other. I understood that I could not hear God’s purpose for me because of my lack of devotion to Him. As I read the Word, I was convinced I had to choose. Thus, I ended my relationship with Robert because he would not accept my conversion.

It was the Holy Spirit directing me to 2 Corinthians 6:14, which explained that I should not be in a personal relationship with an unbeliever. I became convicted and realized that I should not be in a relationship with Robert since my conversion had rendered us unequally yoked. In other words, we were no longer headed in the same direction. Now that my relationship with the Savior was no longer compromised, I was able to continue my transition from conversion to discipleship. This action started me on a true faith walk with the Lord, and I began my season of Him emptying me out. The Word speaks of not putting new wine in a bottle on top of old wine because the new wine ferments, causing the bottle to burst. Our old ways must move out so that the new ways of Christ can move in. Jesus did not want to patch me up; He wanted to make me new. Everything about me had to be new as He worked towards His promise to restore me and preserve me (Matthew 9:17).

After that revelation of surrender, God opened His Word to me like a flood. Whenever I read the Word, interpretation poured out of me. The Holy Spirit always showed up as I filled my journals with His plan and purpose for my life. During one of my devotional periods, the Lord spoke to me and told me to study His Word. I said, "I am studying your Word, Lord."

He said, "No. Study to teach My Word." I heard it, but I did not hear it. I continued to read His Word, study it, and pray.

Then, one Sunday morning, I was sitting in Sunday school as usual, waiting for class to start. The only problem was that our teacher, who was always on time, had not yet arrived. As I sat with about 15 other students waiting, Superintendent Pearl came over and informed us that Teacher Pam was running late. She asked me to start devotion. Like I did every Sunday, I read the focus scripture for the lesson and sang a song, and we ended devotion with prayer. When we were done, I was starting back to my seat when Superintendent Pearl came back to the class and directed me to start teaching the lesson. I said, "Start the lesson?"

She said, "Yes! You study your lesson every week, you will do fine."

I stood, announced the text, and taught my first lesson that Sunday.

Teacher Pam showed up 10 minutes into the lesson and motioned for me to continue teaching. At the end of class, Teacher Pam said, "Sebrina, please pray about becoming my co-teacher."

Even though I agreed to pray, I already knew it was God's will. He had already told me to study to teach. On that day, the Lord started me on my journey to teach his word. I walked right into my purpose because I was obedient when He told me to let go of my ungodly relationship with Robert. This example of obedience became a pattern for me as I continued my Christian walk with the Lord. I realized that Christianity was my daily walk because I was now on a journey and not trying to get to a destination in this life. My zeal to always complete the project and achieve my goal had to be laid aside. I finally got it; on this journey, the "well done" does not count on this side. "Well done" means done, which means I cannot hear that acclamation on this side.

Chapter 4
Wanting to Marry

I do not recall having a little girl's fairytale dream of getting married one day. Getting married was inevitable to me since, by my parents' example, that was the only way to have a family. Growing up sheltered, I thought all families consisted of a father, mother, children, and a dog. My earliest memory of understanding the family unit was at the age of five, when we lived in Fort Walton Beach, Florida. There were six of us then: my three older sisters, my younger sister, and my brother. We lived there for three years. During the last year, my youngest brother was born, completing my parents' set of 7 children.

We believed in the adage "The more, the merrier," and we lived it. We did almost everything as a family. As happens in most families, we grew up and developed different personalities, and our interests changed. Playing with the younger children no longer appealed to the older children. That fuzzy feeling that accompanied doing most things together began to unravel as I approached age 16. But my enjoyment of it did not totally leave me. I kept it and thought about it often through the years. Being surrounded by my family provided me with a warm blanket on a cold wintery day. Once I became an adult and moved away from home, I still longed for that fuzzy warm blanket.

Meeting my Husband at 17

The Lord blessed me when He allowed me to connect with a church that ministered to the total person; being in this new circle contributed to my finding myself again. While I was away at school, I learned that I could be in the midst of many people and still feel alone. I longed to be with my family more often than not. My church family really soothed my feelings of emptiness. I was 22 when I gave my life to the Lord and 25 when I totally submitted, having that conversion experience that led me to say yes to God and no to my flesh. That was when I began to beg God for a mate. Yes! I begged God because I wanted a family, I wanted my warm blanket. I wanted that fuzzy feeling again. As I continued to pray and seek God for His will concerning my family life, I told Him what I wanted instead of asking Him what He wanted for me. God is so merciful towards His children in that He gives us what we need and not what we want.

As I previously mentioned, in high school, I was not connected. I was only there to fulfill the requirements for my diploma so I could move on with my plan. What I did not see then was that God was planting seeds for my life. Every day, I spent my lunch period in the library working on my homework assignments because, immediately after school, I would go to work for three hours. One day, while working frantically in the library on an assignment that was due the next day, I was interrupted by one of my classmates. She asked me if she could introduce me to one of her friends. She introduced me to Mark, who I noticed was always in the library at the same time as me. That introduction did not lead to a friendship as we were ending the school year and would be graduating in a month. I inquired about him as I spoke to a few other girls in my class. They told me he was known as the "preacher boy." He wore suits to school and carried a Bible along with his books. Mark took the opportunity to speak to me again at our senior luncheon. He also invited me to take a photo with him with his Polaroid camera. He took four pictures and gave me two (I still have those photos today). The next week, senior week, Mark approached me again and asked me to sign his memory book, and he signed mine. He wrote a note that read, *"To a beautiful young lady who I don't know very well, but hope later in life, our friendship will grow,"* and he put his phone number above his signature in parentheses. I read it and thought, "That's nice." I never called him because I was taught nice girls did not initiate calls to boys.

The next time I saw Mark and engaged in an actual conversation with him was five years later. Our paths crossed while I was on my way to Mercy Hospital for an appointment. He was working across the street at Michael Reese Hospital. We talked long enough to give each other quick updates on our lives but did not exchange contact information. Three years later, our paths crossed again. This time, we connected while on the bus one February morning, so it was very cold, and I was all bundled up beyond recognition, yet he recognized me and called me by name. He said, "Hi Sebrina. Mark, from King High School."

Responding, I said, "I know who you are."

Our conversation was cut short due to the crowding on the bus: He was standing, and I was sitting. We ended our conversation with "Nice seeing you again." But, this time, Mark would not let me get away. As the bus emptied, he and I were still on it. He came over and asked to sit next to me. We talked all the way to our stop, which was the end of the line. Again, another "God thing." He worked across the street from where I worked, so he invited me to lunch to continue our conversation. We met at the bus depot, where we shared as we sat on the bench, eating our lunch. This time, I gave him my telephone number. No, I still did not take his number.

We went on a few dates before I took his number. About a month later, we shared our senior class memory books and yearbooks from school. At the same time, we both fixed our eyes on the sentiment he had written in my memory book. It jolted us as we had both forgotten what he had written. I almost dropped the book when I realized God was blessing Mark with his desire to become friends with me as he had expressed it in my book 10 years previously. After ending our date that evening, we did not speak to each other or see each other for two months. My candid conversation about praying and asking God to direct us in our friendship was too much for him, or so I thought. I was stunned after I read in the Bible that, "He that finds a wife finds a good thing. . . (Proverb 18:22). "Am I Mark's good thing?" I wondered.

I Surrender My Plan for Yours

As I was waiting to hear from God, I cried out to Him, asking for peace. In my conversation with God that night, I told Him that if it was His will that I remain single, I would accept it, but I needed his peace and comfort. I told God I would no longer allow myself to be distracted from seeking His will, looking over my shoulder for my mate to show up. I would wait for Him to send Him to my door with red roses. I told God I trusted Him as he knew my address, telephone number, and daily routine. I went to bed early that night, exhausted from crying out to God. Before I got into bed, I got on my knees and asked the Lord for a hug. I slept peacefully until the phone rang. As I pulled myself out of my sleep and answered the phone, the voice on the other end said, "Hello, Sebrina? This is Mark." He said, "First I want to apologize for not being in contact with you for the past months. I want to talk to you, but not over the phone. Is it possible for me to come over for about an hour?"

I thought about it for a minute and agreed. My mind began to run with planning. All while I was dressing and taking my rollers out of my hair, I was planning a script of what I would say to him. He was detained by his mother and ended up arriving an hour later than he had said. I became frazzled, believing this was a test and I had failed. When he arrived an hour late, I could no longer recall the script I had planned. So, I sat and listened as he shared from his heart. The more he talked, the more I was able to relax and surrender the mumbled script in my head. He shared how, when he read the note in my memory book, the Lord spoke to him.

He felt he did not have his life together, so he needed to go seek direction from God. He saw me as a real-deal Christian woman and did not want to mess up my life by not following the Lord's instructions to resolve some issues before starting the relationship. He said that, two months after following the Lord's instructions, he asked God for a wife. The Lord spoke my name into his spirit. He delayed calling me all day, seeking God for the right words. Mark asked me in a straightforward manner if we could spend time together with the goal of marrying. I agreed. Keeping his word, he thanked me for allowing him to visit that evening. As he opened the door to leave, he turned and said, "Can I have a hug?" We exchanged a brotherly hug, and he left.

As I was preparing for bed all over again, I recalled my request of the Lord for a hug: "That was my hug!" The break in our friendship had not just been for Mark. It had also been for me to surrender that area of my life to God, allowing His plan to replace mine.

Committed to Me

My medical issues had not subsided. I was still very sickly. Our dates consisted of him picking me up for church, taking me to doctor appointments, and grabbing a late lunch or early dinner. Soon after we started dating, my medical condition worsened, causing me to have surgery. Most of my immediate family had left the Chicago area, so I did not have family support; however, my mother came to town to care for me the first two weeks after my discharge from the hospital. After Mom left, friends visited me regularly to check on me. One day, my friend, Mrs. Pam came by to spend the afternoon with me.

During our visit, I shared Mark's sentiment to me in my memory book. I told her I was waiting on God to say yes as he had already shared that his intentions were to marry me. I told her that I had asked God to let the man I was to marry bring me red roses to my door. As we were chatting at the dining room table, the doorbell rang. Mrs. Pam turned to look out the window. Not wanting me to spoil the surprise, she said, "Sebrina, do not get up. I will get the door." When Mark walked in, he was carrying a floral arrangement: six red roses with baby's breath. Once again, my mouth fell open. I knew it was God, I just had not expected Him to answer so quickly. Although I agreed to a future engagement at our initial reunion visit, we soon made it an official engagement and got married 10 months later.

Now that we were married, I saw myself in a whole new light. My husband became my mirror. Everything in the Bible that I had been reading, studying, and teaching was now reflecting, and truth was being revealed. The Word revealed through Mark that I was a controlling little woman. Now 29, I had been single and on my own for the previous 10 years. I thought that the fuzzy feeling I had been looking for would return immediately upon marriage. Instead, I felt like my life had been invaded. It was difficult submitting to "and two shall become one." While I had been studying it and teaching it, it had sounded like violin music playing, and now it was a combination of the bass and snare drum, along with the cymbals, all playing out of turn. I thought I was prepared for marriage and believed I was, but just not ready to submit. I should probably unpack that statement by saying I had all the tools for marriage: I was mature and had an established relationship with Christ; I even had a bonus in that I had seen my mother submit to my father in their marriage.

My problem was that I had not considered what submitting to my husband would look like for me. Yes, this is a "tell the truth, shame the devil" kind of statement. If we were *all* honest, we would admit we had a moment or two in our marriages of pushing back against submission, especially those of us who had married after establishing a career and spending an extended time considering only ourselves.

In my case, some stuff was just pure pride, selfishness, and stubbornness. My parents had given it everything they had, trying to rid me of the character trait of thinking it was my way or the highway. As Daddy had put it, "Sebrina, there is more than one way to skin a cat. Your way is not the only way." I intentionally did the same thing the same way because it was safe, and I would try to push my way onto everyone else. Hindsight will get us straight every time in our pursuit to rebuild our character. We were born into sin, having no fruit. We depend on the Spirit to work the good stuff in us upon salvation.

That perfection thing that emerged in my 20s followed me right into my marriage at 29. Perfectionism was such a part of me until I thought it was a good quality and a necessary part of my character. Unexpectedly, that very character trait was the thing that set us back in the first months of our marriage. One morning, as we were getting ready for church, I noticed Mark's shirt was a little wrinkled from hanging in a crowded closet. I insisted that he let me iron the wrinkles out, but he proceeded to iron the shirt himself. After completing his shirt, he grabbed my dress to press out the wrinkles generated by the same scenario. Upon finishing my dress, he laid it on the bed. I came into the room, noticed the dress still had winkles, and, without thinking, I proceeded to put it back on the ironing board and press it again. Mark watched my entire effort, hanging his head in disappointment. He said, "Oh, my ironing is not good enough for you!"

At that moment, it occurred to me what I had done to my husband. In trying to redeem a big mistake, I said, "It's fine, honey! I just noticed another wrinkle in the front."

It was too late; his interpretation was etched in: "My ironing is not good enough for her." That day, I set my marriage back by allowing my need to be perfect to override an opportunity to show my husband love and appreciation. It was selfish of me not to put away my pride, wear that dress just the way he had ironed it, and enjoy the fuzzy feeling that my husband had taken extra care to help me get dressed that morning.

My need for perfectionism evolved as I tried to meet the high expectations set by my father, "the military man." In our earliest years, my father had instilled in my siblings and I the importance of doing our best. Because I honored my father, I took that expectation seriously, attaching it to everything I did. As I grew from a teenager into a full-grown adult, I kept pushing a little harder to get things as perfect as I could. Eventually, it became unhealthy striving. As I learned God's word, the Lord showed me that, if I accepted Him as a perfect Savior, there was no need for me to strive for perfection. Perfection came in honoring my Savior and being obedient to His instruction. If I did what He said how He said it and when He said to do it, I would be perfect in Him. Acts 17:28a says, "It is in Him we live and move and have our being." It tells me I cannot be perfect in and of my own strength. I read it, and I comprehended it. But it took time to live it as I continued to fail test after test, mimicking a behavior I thought had been a pertinent part of my character since my earliest years. The Word is a master transformer. I am continuing to be transformed by His Word.

Chapter 5
My Plan, Not His

It is true that we make plans and God makes decisions. I remember answering our Pastor's question in pre-marital counseling when he asked us how many children we wanted. I blurted out four. I did not consult God; I just believed that, once we got married, it was God's will that we grow a family.

Before accepting the Lord and acknowledging Him as Lord of my life, I had already planned my life. I struggled to follow the Lord's lead in many areas, one being instructions for my physical health. Type 2 diabetes and fibroid tumors shook my world, leading me to a place of devastation when I had to face a diagnosis of infertility. I shut down because I realized that I had not listened to the Holy Spirit years before, when he had moved me to let go of my food addictions to return to good health.

I remembered getting introduced to fasting. I'd read scripture after scripture about spiritual fasting as well as materials on fasting for natural healing. I'd studied with knowledgeable natural healing coaches. I'd had so much information that it had become overwhelming to follow a plan. I had not committed to information I'd learned in the natural healing class, "Heal Thyself." That class had been helpful and simple to follow, but I had not used the material to my benefit. You could say I had packed all that information in and become constipated with it.

I remembered detoxifying my body through a 10-day water fast, after learning proper fasting techniques (Afua, 1993). After acknowledging what Paul had said in Romans 7, I had not taken heed. I'd made a god out of food because I had believed it sustained me more than God. What hurt the most was my missing God's instructions to "heal myself." He'd told me to get my body ready because He'd known my heart's desire to bear children. He'd also seen me headed for disaster due to the way I was abusing my body with food. He'd sent word that the flood was coming. When He'd seen my aloofness, He'd sent me a knock at the door. As I'd began to drown in sickness, He'd sent me a rescue boat, and I still had not gotten into the boat. Then the first surgery had come, and he'd sent me a helicopter. I had still declined a ride to safety. Now, in my infertility diagnosis, I was drowning and expecting God to have mercy and save me. When He did not save me from the diagnosis, I got angry, not with Him, but with myself. As a result, I walked in secret self-condemnation for years. The Lord allowed me to hear His word over and over in my heart: that my old way of selfish living was not my demise. I was still victorious over my sins because He had borne them on the cross. The Bible tells me to repent and not to carry the guilt (Romans 7:23-8:1). In my repentance, I continued to beg God for a child.

I went from my plan of wanting four children to just wanting ***a*** child, to be specific, an infant child. After looking at adoption, we quickly dismissed that idea as all the variables did not add up. This, too, was not God's plan for us. Again, I begged and bargained with God, thinking He would perform a miracle in my body as a testimony. He responded to my begging by showing me yet another way in which our plan still was not His plan. He had already decided for us that we would raise a child. The Lord, in His mercy, blessed us with a child, just not an infant child. My husband and I assumed responsibility for our niece and raised her from age 13. We poured into her for 10 years. We needed her as much as she needed us. Pouring into her soothed that pain of wanting an infant, and that desire soon left.

Raising her was fulfilling for both of us. I have so many memories of moments with her that taught us all valuable life lessons. Those disciplinary moments revealed how much we loved each other. We learned, in disciplining her, that we had to be disciplined ourselves. God's plan always trumped our plan. Surrendering our own plan for His was difficult while we were going through it, but, in hindsight, we were thankful for His display of love towards us as He favored us through it all.

Chapter 6
Transforming Me

Transformation, whether simple or dramatic, involves change. The most familiar example of physical transformation is that of a caterpillar changing into a butterfly. I imagine this transformation is easy because it is natural. It is an expected change because nature performs it, and we accept it.

Even though I had lost 90 pounds, I was considered obese based on the body mass index (BMI) charts. After working with my personal trainer and my nutritionist for five years; I lost weight, and the Lord allowed me to keep it off. When I became more mature in the spirit and connected to the Holy Spirit, I heard His whisper to "get the weight off" and was moved immediately to heed His directions. His instructions were still the same. The Lord, He changes not (Malachi 3:6) I had all the instructions that had been recorded in my head; all I needed to do was "repent." I had received the same instructions many times before. This time, I desired transformation; I wanted a change.

I immediately committed to a regular exercise regimen along with a change in my eating habits. Getting used to a regular exercise routine was not difficult because of my goal-oriented nature, and the workout regimen designed specifically for me was helpful. Soon after I incorporated cardio and weight training, the weight began to fall off. Another key was accountability. I had a scheduled appointment for my workout two times a week and an appointment with my nutritionist once a week that involved food prep discussion and a weigh-in. It was keeping the weight off that challenged me due to the "real weight" I was carrying that had nothing to do with my physical body.

I got to morbid obesity by living in denial for 10 years between 30 and 45. During that 15-year period, as I suffered with many health problems, I did whatever I had to do to alleviate the presentation problem. My health problems, which drove me to think about weight loss, hindered me from engaging in childbearing. This started me on the pursuit of numerous fad diets. If it was called a diet, I tried it. I tried the cabbage diet, the peanut butter and grapefruit diet, the low carbohydrate diet, a fasting diet, and a high-protein diet, only to receive the worse diagnoses of type II diabetes, high blood pressure, and elevated cholesterol.

The wake-up call came when my doctor announced I needed to start an insulin regimen to maintain my blood sugar. This recommendation came after the discovery of extremely high blood sugar readings during my annual examination at 33. Understanding the doctor's diagnosis, I declined her recommendation and opted to get serious about my diet and exercise program. She met me halfway by prescribing an oral medication that immediately regulated my dangerously high sugar levels and suggested a strict eating plan for six months.

Two months went by as I followed this strict diet. I lost little weight. Considering I had given up my comfort foods, I was discouraged by these results. At my three-month checkup, I shared my food journal, which charted my daily food choices, with my doctor. When she reviewed my food choices for my daily meals and snacks, she determined my food intake was poor, causing a shutdown of my metabolism. My poor food choices were sending signals to my body that I was starving it. Although there was weight loss, it was much too little, considering my activities. I was starving myself all day, and binge eating in the evenings.

She explained the need to eat based on the food pyramid (which consisted of the four food groups) and to eat my largest meal for breakfast. I also followed her recommendation to take an intentional walk every day for 30 minutes. Following her recommended diet and exercise plan, I lost 12 pounds the next month. Once my body became acclimated to my new regimen, I shifted to a high-impact workout. Within six months, I lost over 30 pounds. Now that there was noticeable weight loss, I was motivated to keep going. Ironically, I was doing a more intense workout, eating more food than prescribed, and still losing a considerable amount of weight at each weigh-in. At my month-six doctor's visit, my doctor removed the recommendation for insulin from my chart and reduced my oral medications as well.

Today, I no longer consume medication for diabetes as I made my new eating and exercise regimen a lifestyle change that allowed me to totally eliminate medication. It took me five years to transition from a sickly body at 272 pounds to a healthy body at a proportional weight. Yes, I have to work daily to keep it off. My weight is up sometimes and down at other times, depending upon the season of my life. I have freed myself from the bondage of daily weigh-ins that allowed the scale to dictate my success. I maintain my weight by allowing myself a 10-pound slide and only weighing myself once per week. It works for me! This is part of my personal commitment to take responsibility for my health.

I am sure there are other success stories that yielded similar results to mine, but I can only attest to my experience. It was not the Lord's will that I become diabetic. Rather, my disobedience led to that. I share with friends and family regularly, recommending diet and exercise as the solution to any health problem. Some people are born with certain birth defects and deficiencies that require more work to resolve, but many common health issues like high blood pressure, diabetes, and high cholesterol can be resolved with deliberate corrections in diet and exercise. It is like shifting in reverse, turning around to drive in the opposite direction. It is a matter of repentance! Some things I completely stopped eating, others I learned to eat in moderation. I replaced my 80% sugary diet with fresh fruits and vegetables. I also choose water over sugary drinks as our bodies function best when we consume water at a volume that is half our body weight in ounces. I am not always successful, but I make a serious attempt daily.

One of the biggest struggles along my journey was making time to exercise. The solution I found involved putting my workout time in my calendar as a stable part of my weekly routine. Writing things down was powerful as it moved me closer to a commitment. I am motivated to stay the course because my new regimen allowed me to eliminate four of the five medications I was taking daily. Overall, I reduced my BMI, which allowed me to abandon a diagnosis of obesity, diabetes, and elevated cholesterol, thus preserving my life.

Chapter 7
Returning to School

I am not sure if everyone in this life experiences a real "mid-life" crisis, or if there is such a thing as a "mid-life" crisis? How does one determine if they are going through or having one? To me *mid-life* suggests the middle of your life. If we do not know the lengths of our life spans, how can we really determine the midway points? I am going to refer to these suggested midway points as "milestone markers."

In planning my life, I sorted out what life events I wanted to happen and when. I thought I should accomplish certain things at certain points in my life based on what I saw growing up. According to my philosophy, I was supposed to finish school and land a career by age 22 (my first milestone marker). I was supposed to get married, buy a home, and birth our first child by age 25 (missing this one was the most devastating). For my timeline to work, I was supposed to have four children by 30 and assume the role of wife and mother by staying at home until age 40, at which time I would reenter the workforce to help secure a nest egg for the children's education. I could see God laughing right there.

Where did those concepts come from? They came from watching my parents, who always provided us with sufficient housing and all the amenities to make it a home. My mother was always present; she was the first person I saw when I woke up in the morning and the last person I saw before I fell asleep at night. She stood in the doorway as the bus pulled up to drop my siblings and I home from school. She prepared every meal and graded every school paper before I handed it in to the teacher. She taught me how to sort, wash, fold, and put away my laundry. She was the one that told me about my body before the health teacher did. Mother was always there, so the plan was for me, along with my husband, to mimic the same. I was the fourth child of seven, and I figured I had not turned out so bad, so maybe four children would be a good number.

Age 22 had come and gone, along with age 25. I remember getting a call from my Auntie on my 25th birthday. She greeted me with a "Happy Birthday, **my niece**!" In return, I cried, shedding tears that expressed less than joy. When she asked what was wrong, I responded by telling her I could not believe I was 25 with no "real" accomplishments. After laughing my tears dry, she counseled me, explaining how blessed I was and that I was right where God wanted me to be. She told me to let Him be the driver and enjoy the ride. That was the problem; I did not know how to yield the driver's seat and relinquish control. This need to be in control resulted from the absence of my father. Once he was no longer there to take care of everything, I felt I needed to take over.

After accepting Christ, I did not relinquish that control until He taught me 1 Peter 5:7. I did not get it right away, but, when I did, I felt the weight of the world lift off my shoulders. I learned to cast all my cares on Him and trusted that He cared for me as my Heavenly Father.

Getting married at 29, age 30 was right on my heels. According to my plan, I was already behind. As the fixer syndrome emerged in me, I felt like I needed to redeem the time lost. I started pondering a plan to get my body ready for my first pregnancy. Now it was time to get serious about working on my overall health by losing the excess weight. I had already seen some of the best doctors that my insurance could accommodate concerning my female medical issues. I sought them out again, but the story was the same from one doctor to the next: I needed to work on my health issues first.

At 34, hope came when I visited a fertility clinic in Indiana that assured me, after reading my medical records, that its program might yield us a successful outcome. That hope was deflated when I submitted to a glucose test as part of my diagnostic blood work, which suggested I had type 2 diabetes. The doctor said it was too risky to take me through their procedures without stabilizing my blood sugar levels. He suggested I get my blood sugar levels under control and come back. My primary care doctor put me on a medication regimen, and I went on a 40-day fast, which resulted in my losing 42 pounds. I went back to see the infertility specialist and continued to work through the procedures. This time, it was determined that my hormone levels were too low, and I was not a good candidate for the program procedures. Devastated, I went into a silent depression.

After 10 years of my hope going up and down, I wanted to be alone to process this finality. I really wanted to curl up in a fetal position and hide, but I had to keep moving. I had my niece to care for, I wanted to be present in my relationship with my husband, and I wanted to keep fulfilling my calling as a teacher. It was a heavy load for me to process and keep moving. So, without processing my pain, I picked myself up and continued with life. The Lord sustained me in His Word as I experienced more heartbreak. Daddy's death had been the first instance of heartbreak, and here was another. Both were equally painful. I remember feeling limp and wondering how long I could keep standing. At times, I felt like I could not breathe.

I was moving towards no longer teaching because I was so overwhelmed with hurt that I could no longer hide it, and pain had become my countenance. Before I could make the final decision, I got a handwritten letter from the First Lady of our church. She shared a testimony given in one of her Sunday school classes by one of my former students. She said the woman told the class, "*I thank God for Teacher Sebrina teaching me the ACTS of PRAYER, because it taught me how to pray, and I no longer struggle with prayer.*" In the letter, she told me to stay on the wall and not to stop building because my teaching was not in vain. That was another God thing as she had no idea what I had just gone through and what I was resolving to do concerning teaching. I picked up the Word again, got my momentum back, and went on. But I still had not released the pain that continued to weigh me down.

Then I was in my late 40s, and age 50 was upon me. It was another milestone marker, causing me to evaluate my life. I still had not finished school. I was raising a teenager and developing my career, yet I was feeling less than accomplished as my 50-year milestone marker approached. Life was not as bad as I made it out to be, but the absence of a degree gave me a feeling of failure. This was an expectation I had latched onto in my earlier years, so it lay in my mind as an incomplete task. Even though Daddy was no longer living, I wanted to fulfill that expectation. While renewing efforts to have an infant child was not a realistic goal, surely, a degree was obtainable. When I posed the idea to my husband, with very little contemplation, he disagreed and suggested I relax and concentrate on my career. I remember my disappointment and unwillingness to accept that response.

About a month after our conversation, our Pastor preached a sermon, "When the husband becomes the help-meet." I remember the congregation chuckling at the announcement of the sermon title. I did not chuckle but moved to the edge of my seat. My husband and I had had another intense conversation the previous week as I had presented the idea of completing my degree again. Again, he had decided for both of us that it was not a good idea since I was settled in my career, and completing my education was not a do-or-die decision. I remember leaving the conversation hurt and disappointed and wanting to rebel when the Lord soothed me with a "hold on" response.

This sermon perked up my spirit as I recalled the Lord's acclamation to "wait," and a glimpse of hope flooded my heart. WOW! Pastor's opening statement said, "Husbands, it is your responsibility to ensure your wives reach their full potential. Whether she is at home taking care of the kids or out working, helping you secure your family's financial future, you must make sure she has all the tools to be successful." I stood up and worshipped with tears streaming down my face as the Spirit bore witness that this was my message of hope and redemption. At the end of the message, the Pastor had the husbands vow to their wives that they would listen to what their hearts said regarding how they could help them become their best selves. My husband turned to me with a cuddling embrace and said, "*I guess we are going back to school, honey.*" And we did! He took up the slack. Whatever I left undone to get my assignments, papers, and presentations done, he stepped in and completed.

This was certainly another "God thing" that had been brewing in my spirit since I'd abandoned it at age 20, only I'd never addressed it and it had continued to sit in the back of my mind. Now it was in the forefront of my mind, and thoughts ran through my mind as I began reconstructing a plan. God already had a plan. In the weeks following, a sister in Christ that was enrolled in school asked me to accompany her to an "open house" event at her university. I agreed to go with no hesitation, certainly not expecting to get my own needs met concerning my goal to complete my degree, but God blessed me in my willingness to go. The counselor that met with us concerning my friend's curriculum also assisted me. She shared with me the different programs offered by the university, including an alternative adult degree program.

As a result of meeting the woman at the university on that day, I received a phone call the following week, inviting me to apply for the REACH program. The application process involved making an appointment to take a writing test. The writing test consisted of choosing one of many subjects and producing a 250-to-500-word essay in one hour. The test was done on a computer program that gave an immediate result upon completion. Within 10 minutes of my hitting "submit," the administrator came into the room, offered me an application for enrollment, and said, "We can enroll you today as your score is in the 90th percentile; that automatically waives your enrollment fee." It was the end of December, and classes would be starting in two weeks. My head was spinning; I did not know how to respond. God had done what I'd asked Him to do, but I had not gotten a chance to think about it and put my plan in place. God had taken control of everything and had not needed my help. Thank God I'd submitted to His plan. I enrolled in classes, ordered my books, and began preparing for my first session. True to form, He immediately ushered me into His plan, so I did not have time to contemplate how I was going to incorporate my plan in derailing His. What a mighty God! As always, His plan was not only better, but perfect!

The REACH program was designed for seasoned adults who wanted to return to school after establishing families and careers. The foundation of the program afforded them the opportunity to use and possibly gain credit for the knowledge, skills, and abilities they'd gained through the years from their life experiences. The program was very attractive to me because I had already played in so many different arenas; I felt like I had already earned many degrees in the school of hard knocks. In the REACH program, each cohort course lasted 12 weeks. During each 12-week course, I read four to six books, articles, and journals and listened to lectures that filled in the gaps and taught me concepts I had not grasped from my life experiences. The beauty of the program was its Christian-based platform. Each professor displayed a relationship with Jesus Christ. They were people like me, loving God and wanting to see the body of Christ rise to its full potential. Some were pastors and some psychologists; all held master's degrees and doctorates.

During the introduction of each class, the professors usually gave their salvation testimonies. It was very exciting listening to such phenomenal spirit-filled teachings while gaining a degree. I was so tickled in my spirit each week as I studied and produced projects, speeches, and paper after paper on which the professors wrote comments such as "Excellent manuscript." I did not think they were so great because, most times, I just submitted exactly what the instructions asked me to do: no more, no less. At the end of the course, to prove I had grasped the course concepts and had properly interpreted the required books and articles, I was required to produce a 12-page paper. In each paper, I had to integrate a Christian worldview, self-knowledge, open-minded perspectives, critical thinking, artistic appreciation, and organizational effectiveness and to communicate evidence of lifelong learning.

I viewed each paper as my most prized challenge at the end of each course. While most students dreaded this activity, I welcomed it as I compiled notes, articles, and handouts in anticipation of completing my paper throughout the 12-week course. The research was the most rewarding as I got to analyze Bible verses, learning more and more about myself as the Spirit revealed it. These writings contributed to my healing process, which the Lord was leading me to as an answer to my prayer for healing.

After completing the first course, I met with a guidance counselor to map out the required courses to complete the program. My initial meeting determined that I needed five years to complete the program. This was determined by applying the 60 hours earned from previous course work at two other universities. While I was speaking with the guidance counselor, she asked me if I had any life experiences that coincided with courses in my degree plan that I could organize in a portfolio. Upon researching coursework I'd studied in a previous counseling course and on-the-job training received, I was able to produce papers proving I had grasped the course concepts of subjects outlined in my degree plan to satisfy my degree requirements. My completed portfolio was approved in the first submission, securing me 22 credit hours and allowing me to satisfy my program requirements two years early to complete my degree.

I finished my degree in a new body in May 2015, graduating with honors. I remember taking pictures as we celebrated in the crowd. I held my diploma cover in my hand, posing for the picture, and my husband grabbed the other end of the cover, leaning in as if it were his. He was so right in his gesture as it was just as much his as mine: Without him, I would not have completed my degree. It was such a satisfying feeling completing that lifelong goal. While completing my degree, I was able to suppress my state of depression as I still had not dealt with those issues. Working on my coursework was another way I escaped my pain.

I, like so many other women (from all walks of life), carry hurts from the punches of life. When God saved me, He first saved me from hellfire, but He also saved me from myself. I have struggled with perfectionism all my adult life. This need for perfection grew out of my need to be in control. My need for control comes from a place of hidden pain: my father leaving me in death after just turning 18 years old, failing at my first attempt to complete my degree, and a failed plan to have children after marriage. I ate a lot of sugary foods as I allowed sugar to comfort me in my feelings of defeat. Most times, my choice of sugary food was ice cream. Ice cream was one of those foods that our parents used to reward us with. I enjoyed that soothing sensation of a creamy bowl of ice cream fixing anything right into my adult years. It became my drug of choice. I ate ice cream when I was glad, when I was sad, when I was celebrating, and even when disappointed.

One reason why I chose ice cream was the memory behind it. I had many memories of eating ice cream with my family, particularly Daddy. He had really enjoyed a creamy bowl of ice cream. He delighted in sharing ice cream with us around the table and, sometimes, as a treat when we all watched a family movie. I recalled that, each time one of us had a birthday, we got to choose our ice cream and cake flavor. Mom would bake our cake, and Daddy would bring the five-quart container of ice cream home after work. He said we didn't need to have a party; we were the party. That was how my siblings and I developed such close relationships: We spent more time with each other than with our friends. Daddy would always say, "Blood is thicker than water." He explained that statement by saying friendships should not replace our relationships with our siblings. I attribute to that teaching my closeness to all my siblings. I cherish my relationships with my siblings. Each relationship soothes an emptiness in my heart from the past.

Whenever we have family gatherings, ice cream is almost always on the menu. It is not that I cannot give up ice cream: I can do all things through Christ that strengthens me (Philippians 4:13). It is one of those things I choose not to give up but do in moderation instead. Having a bowl of creamy ice cream is like having a date with Daddy and spending time with my family.

I covered my pain for so many years that even the people closest to me did not know it existed. I built a thick wall around my heart to ensure I would never experience another heartbreak like the previous two. I did not think I could sustain another blow like losing Daddy.

Chapter 8
Unmasking Me

For three years in a row, beginning in 2018, I was hit with a different illness in the first quarter of the year. As I thought about it, I knew it was not a coincidence but an attention-getter from God. The first year, I let it go. It did not capture my attention, but when I got sick the following year, it raised an eyebrow. As had been the case during the first year of its occurrence, the doctors could not diagnose my illness. I studied the Word as I sought answers from the Lord. I wanted to know why, after submitting and achieving a healthier me, I would get sick now. Most times, when I get to the end of my reasoning and things still do not add up, I pass them off by saying, "God's business; I will wait until He speaks to me." This time, I felt helpless as I waited. Through the years, I have learned my comfort comes from finding the Romans 8:28 in all situations. In each sickness, He just said, "You need help! Accept the help. Let go of 'it' and accept the help."

I thought, "What is the 'it'?"

He said, "Let go of thinking you have to do everything on your own." The Lord told me he was working in me to do His good pleasure (Philippians 2:13). He revealed to me that "it" was a pride issue. Letting go of the pride required taking off the mask. That was difficult because I had been wearing a mask for a long time, not allowing Jesus to help me. I quoted the Bible, and I taught the Bible, but now God was calling me to act on it. I exhaled in relief because I was tired of carrying the weight of that protective shield around my heart. On the exterior, I had the appearance of strength and usually upheld that strong woman demeanor. But, on the inside, I was an image of weakness even though I was moving towards my complete healing. As strong women not willing to admit it, many of us become a source of comfort for others but suffer in silence with our own past hurts and current hurts. We help others out of our own need to be healed. This is the work of the Lord, working both to will and to do of His good pleasure (Philippians 2:13). In this season, God healed my hurt, restoring my heart.

How Did I Break Through the Pain?

I hid my pain by putting on a front until it became unbearable. Years ago, I heard an evangelist say, "We usually do not change until the pain of staying the same becomes unbearable." I remember hearing the call of God like it was yesterday and feeling His tug at my heart. But instead of releasing my pain to Him, I tried to deal with it myself since I was a "strong woman." My new relationship with Jesus saved me because I no longer suffered in silence. I had a friend in Jesus. I had inherited the privilege of carrying everything to Him in prayer, only I did not take advantage of my special privilege. I remember that, three years after I gave my heart to Christ while in my mid-20s, He invited me to sup with Him. During my special prayer time with Him, the Lord woke me up between three and four every morning during the fourth prayer watch. This prayer watch is the last prayer watch of the night. The prayers were powerful. They ushered me into my day as I allowed God to direct it. Presently, I find this time to be the most effective prayer time for me in seeking the Lord inside and outside crisis. I would pour out my heart to Him, and, after prayer, my heart was always lifted. During those times with Jesus, I received my deepest emotional healing. I remember a matriarch Deacon at my church praying, "Lord, here we are, wounded and sad, but thank God we can find a resting place in You."

I whispered to the Lord, "Where is that place? I need to find that place."

Then the Lord began to whisper to me in my spirit regularly, "Come to me, Sebrina, heaviness and all, and I will give you rest." But I continued to hide. In my hiding, the hurt got more deeply imbedded in my heart until, one day, I broke. It was to the first illness that I submitted. He wanted me to write what He had said. Not what He was saying, but what He had said. I was looking for what God was preparing to give me when I should have been looking at what He had already given me. Everything I needed; God had already given me. He had given it to me during those early morning prayer sessions.

He Answered My Prayer

I prayed a specific prayer to the Lord during my special prayer time years ago. I prayed that He would not only heal me but HHHe would make me whole. I prayed this prayer based on God's Word, which said, *"He is not a man that he can lie, what he said he will do, he will do just that"* (Numbers 23:19). The problem was I had not done my part. Psalm 84:11 says, "*He is my sun and shield; He is gracious towards me, and no good thing will He withhold from me if I walk upright."* God kept his part as he protected me through the years, even when I was not walking right and rejected his plan for my life.

When I retired from my career after working for 36 years, I entered into unintended solitude. The solitude described in the Bible is a state of being alone. It is a state in which one intends to be alone with God. In this type of solitude, I would have found rest, enjoyment, and rediscovery of myself. However, I did not enter this type of solitude. Mine was unintended solitude as I found myself alone in a state of depression. I spent time alone trying to sort out my life and somehow managed to lose perspective. I was in an unfamiliar place, asking myself daily, "How did I get here?"

I kept asking Jesus to come and get me, save me from myself. His response was Psalm 46:10: "*Be still and know that I am God*."

I suddenly got flashbacks because, in the three years leading up to that point, that had been His constant response to my prayers. It had become my doodle. I had written it everywhere: in the margins of my journals, on notepads, and even in the margins of sermon notes and lessons I'd prepared. I could not comprehend that simple instruction because I felt like I was already being still. It was my prayer partner who spoke in prayer, saying that I needed to turn off the MP3 player in my head. I had confused being still in my body with being still in my mind and spirit. I was always on the go, seeking to get something done that I thought was necessary. God was beckoning me to come to Him for rest, an unrestricted rest, but I would only rest for a moment because moving at a constant pace kept me going, or so I thought.

God did not give me additional instructions until I completed the instructions, He had already given me. He said, "Let go of the hurt. Give it to me." Because I had carried my hurts for so long, they had become a part of me, and I did not know how to just "let go." He spoke to me: "On the other side of letting go is the answer to your prayer, Sebrina, a place of wholeness." That was what the wellness journey was all about, an avenue to get me to that wholeness.

Chapter 9

Journey to Wholeness

I am a very emotional person. If emotions can be passed down from one generation to another, I believe I got my emotionalism from Daddy. Daddy was very emotionally expressive. He always greeted you with a kiss, gave hearty handshakes and great bear hugs. He did not meet you as a stranger; he showed care and concern for anyone he met. He was very confident and as open-hearted with his feelings as I am.

I am always eager to share a story, especially if I believe it will help somebody. He was an emotional man and saw no shame in shedding a tear; still, he was a strong man, an honorable man. I remember asking God to lessen my emotions because it seemed they would always get the best of me. He responded with a resounding "No!" He said He'd made me that way; I would not be Sebrina without my specific display of emotions. Like my father, I am quick to hug and console. I had to learn how to restrain myself from showing emotional concern in my career. Through this process, I learned how to hide my emotions rather than how to display them properly. This caused me more harm than good because I commenced filing my painful emotions away rather than discarding them; eventually, they became too heavy.

Healing and wholeness are not the same, but they are cousins as they live in the same family, working together toward total restoration. I may have desired healing in my body due to my emotional pain, but I desired wholeness because I wanted peace in my heart. I wanted to be free from the emotional pain I'd held on to and neglected to surrender after repeated beckoning from the Lord. I knew this peace was available; but pride caused me to refuse it. Ironically, wholeness is completeness, a kind of "perfection," only, it is being perfect in Christ. I see it as a positional perfection in which I am perfect as I position myself in God. Hebrews 10:14 says, *"I am sanctified in Him as I offer myself in sacrifice to Him in all things."* Only in Him can I reach my goal of perfection.

When I finally made the decision to let go of the emotional pain that God had asked me to give to him; it was not a single event. Every time I let go of one form of pain, another emerged. I followed his specific instructions to get free as He took me on a journey involving many avenues that directed me to wholeness. These avenues mostly included

- Exploring natural health and healing
- Accepting my husband's help
- Completing my degree
- Creating scrapbooks
- Raising our niece
- Teaching Sunday school
- Working as a Social Service manager
- Mentoring young adult women.

A two-year weight-loss journey.

He made beauty out of my ashes. As I sat in the mist of mourning, the Lord allowed me to have events of celebration and praise (Isaiah 61:3).

First

He instructed me to get the weight off. My physical weight was literally a hiding place for me. He'd told me several times to get the weight off, but I knew this time that mine would be an act of submission to his directive. This was all the hand of God because, for the first time in my life, it was not as daunting task. I had strength like never before to exercise and deny myself food that was a major contributor to my weight gain. I ate a vegan diet for 10 months to learn how to eat and establish proper eating habits. The Lord allowed me to see, through my nutritionist, that my mind and emotions were tied to the condition of my body. In losing the last 50 pounds on my weight-loss journey, I became free of diabetes medication.

My medical charts now read, "Diabetes is diet-controlled." That accomplishment caused my confidence to soar higher than ever before as I took back my power over my body. According to my nutritionist, diabetes is not an inevitable diagnosis resulting from family history. I did not inherit diabetes from my parents. Diabetes is an imbalance of our blood sugars resulting from our diet. I ate ice cream and the like irresponsibly for years as a source of comfort. I replaced meals with these type foods too frequently, which got me that diabetes diagnosis. It had nothing to do with my Grandparent's, Uncle's or Aunt's diabetes diagnosis. People usually grow up doing what they see their parents doing until they get an awakening. Thank God I got my mine before it was too late. Now I eat ice cream in celebration, not out of need, as I was delivered from the emotional pain that I used to soothe by eating it. *This was my first step out of a place of denial.*

Second

Now that the weight was off, the journey to keep it off began. I decided to face the pain that was hidden behind the weight. Under those 272 pounds were pain and hurt I'd suppressed for years. I mentioned that very statement to a friend, and, without hesitation, she said, "You need to come to Celebrate Recovery." Most people, especially Christians, are first turned off by the name. The name suggests that one needs to have an addiction to be part of "a recovery program." Which a person usually associates with an alcohol or drug problem only. Christians are usually not quick to admit to their hurts, habits, and hang-ups, which are the core issues the Celebrate Recovery program addresses. At the first meeting I attended, I showed up with my guard up, not expecting the "take away" I got. The meeting was phenomenal as it took me to a place of serenity. That night, I left, thanking the Lord for leading and allowing me to totally submit to a new journey in the program.

I participated in the first step study that allowed me to work through steps to address my hurts, habits, and hang-ups. An addiction is a compulsive behavior. Most people are addicted to something, but when it is something acceptable, it is not regarded negatively. I believe every human being should submit to this program on some level. Most people have a hurt, a habit, and/or a hang-up just by virtue of living on this earth and in a body with a soul. Submitting to this program ushered me into *my second step out of a place of denial.*

Third

The first of my three battles with sickness came shortly after I reached my weight-loss goal. I was flying high but still in a state of denial. Although I had dropped the physical weight, I was carrying emotional weight. The doctors could not pinpoint my issue, but God pointed right to it. He directed me to seek emotional help by sending a wise woman to tell me, "Sebrina, sometimes the counselor needs a counselor." I was directed to a Christian therapist through a trusted resource, and my journey to wholeness began as we worked through my layers of emotions, addressing the "real" weight that had weighed me down. Meeting with my therapist weekly was just what I needed to help me lay aside the pride that I had been nudged to let go of years before. I really did not want to accept the fact that I needed help. It took some time to release because of my thinking, "I'm a strong woman. I help others, I don't need help." What folly! This was my final step towards walking out of denial. Repentance is walking away, never to return to that place again.

Chapter 10

Hope That Lies Within

I now understand that wholeness was a journey I needed to take both physically and emotionally to get to my healing. In hindsight, I really did not miss having a date with my natural father as much as I missed my dates with my Heavenly Father. The love of my Heavenly Father was always there. He loves me in spite of me through His kindness, mercy, and grace: *"It is in Him that I live, move and have my being" (Acts 17:28).* Apart from Him, I have no hope. When I allow the Spirit of God to move within me, hope always emerges.

The "real" Christian life is not a picture of perfection; it is not void of pain or struggles; it deals directly with the issue of pain. Pain that pushes us to desire change is designed to draw us to God. His love allows us to "*go through*" pain and not "*stay in*" it. Through this process, "He" makes us perfect in "Him" to do the work "He" has called us to do and is calling us to do according to Ephesians 4:12. Learning the Word of God is processing it intellectually, but knowing the Word is living it within oneself. As I studied the Word to teach it, I focused on understanding it so that I could impart it; but now I know the Word as it floods my heart with hope that I can touch and receive. That's what Jesus taught me in those many 4 am prayer encounters: He put Himself in me little by little so that I could break through the pain of the past and grab hold of the hope for the future that He placed in my heart when I accepted Him as Savior.

How to Have a Daily Date with the Everlasting Father

Set up a space where only you and God meet. Make a recurring date with the Father. Annotate your calendar (make significant people aware of this recurring date so that you will not be disturbed). Keep that space prepared with a Bible, journal, pen, and highlighter. Approach each meeting expecting God to meet you there.

When I meet with God, I go with the expectation that he will speak to me. I am excited every time we meet. It reminds me of the times when I was a child and needed clarity and Daddy helped me by explaining things at my level. The feeling I have when I go to meet God is one of great expectation, knowing that my everlasting Father will always be there and will never stand me up.

Journal Entry
7/25/2020

The Love of God floods my heart as I reflect on Luke 15:20:

> *"And he arose and came to his father. But when he was still a great way off, his father saw him and had compassion, and ran and fell on his neck and kissed him" (NKJV).*

I know my Heavenly Father loves me. God rejoices over my repentance. It does not matter how far away I get from him or for how long. All I have to do is turn around and head back in the right direction. He sees me, stretches out His arms, and welcomes me back home. He accepts my repentance as if I had never turned and walked away in the first place. God, my heavenly Father, has the attribute of patience. He waits patiently for me to come and sit in His presence and sup with Him. He wants and will wait for that daily date. He is always there, waiting to sup with me, because He is loving, patient, and kind. The best date ever is a daily date with our "Everlasting" Father. I just have to show up.

A Prayer for Journeys

Father, In the name of Jesus, bless us on our journeys to healing and wholeness. Bless us to submit to your Word that tells us to come to You, all who are carrying heaven burdens; let us remember that we can rest in You (Matthew 11:28-30).

Let us give in and lay aside every weight that is holding us back from running the race of faith (Hebrews 12:1). Let us come to know You in the stillness of Your presence (Psalm 46:10) and receive help from You in our time of need. Let us realize that You have the total authority to control every area of our lives and "it is in You that we live, move, and have our being" (Acts 17:28).

Father, let us be comforted in knowing, "Nothing can separate us from Your love" (Romans 8:35-39).

Amen!

ENDNOTES

Chapter 3

- Afua, Q. (1993) Heal Thyself: For Health and Longevity (3rd ed.). A & B Books.

Chapter 6

- Body Mass Index, Table 1: https://www.nhlbi.nih.gov/health/educational/lose_wt/BMI/bmi_tbl.htm.

Chapter 7

- www.centralrichardson.com/Four-Steps-of-Prayer-ACTS

- REACH Adult Undergraduate Program: Trinity International University, https://catalog.tiu.edu/previous-catalogs/2018.Trinity International University; 2065 Half Day Road, Deerfield, IL 60015 (847) 945-8800

Chapter 9

- Celebrate Recovery Homepage: https://www.celebraterecovery.com

www.ingramcontent.com/pod-product-compliance
Lightning Source LLC
La Vergne TN
LVHW010106110826

845155LV00028B/506

* 9 7 8 1 9 4 9 0 2 7 6 1 7 *